A CITY
DESTROYING
ITSELF

A CITY DESTROYING ITSELF

An Angry View of New York

by

Richard J. Whalen

illustrations by

FELIKS TOPOLSKI

William Morrow & Co.
New York, 1965

To the memory of
HERBERT SOLOW
—colleague, friend,
New Yorker

Author's Note

The theme of this essay was first stated in an article in the September, 1964, issue of *FORTUNE*. It then seemed a bit extreme, even to Managing Editor Duncan Norton-Taylor, who had inspired the article with a memorandum on how New York struck him—I should say, *wounded* him—on his return from an extended tour of other American cities. From the bountiful store that every New Yorker possesses, but habitually suppresses, I summoned the "outrage" he demanded. And so, while the city stood gleaming around us in the strong, cleansing sunlight of early fall, *FORTUNE* announced that New York was destroying itself.

Now, almost a year later, though the city still stands, the truth of its deep and worsening crisis is widely accepted as self-evident. The New York *Herald Tribune,* in a brilliant illustration of the public service only alert daily journalism can perform, has just concluded a five-month series of articles under the standing head "City in Crisis." Norton-Taylor would be the last person to claim special powers of prescience; but he saw the obvious necessity of describing a situation so plain it had been ignored as commonplace. I am grateful to him for the assignment. Then as now, my approach has been extremely subjective and highly selective. In revising and expanding on my earlier statement, I have made no attempt to modulate the tone (my store of outrage is far from depleted) or to introduce an ingratiating but specious evenhandedness into the discussion. The subject ought to cause us to raise our voices. Inevitably, events will date some references and examples; the way things are going, I fear that time will lend a quality of understatement.

I have talked with several experts in their areas of special knowledge, and have quoted some of them, but this is neither an expert nor a specialized view of the city. It is a view from the streets and sidewalks and subways.

I am grateful to Marion Buhagiar for assisting me in the original research and for checking this manuscript. In the closing pages, I have drawn on material gathered on another assignment by my colleagues, Seymour Freedgood and Eleanor Johnson Tracy. I am indebted to Brooke Alexander, assistant to the publisher of *FORTUNE,* for arranging the details of this project. To my wife, Joan Marie Whalen, who recently researched, typed, and worried her way through a very long book, I extend my astonished but sincere gratitude for her willingness to see me through this one.

—R.J.W.

Sands Point, New York
July, 1965

8

A CITY
DESTROYING
ITSELF

1 All but a few years of my life have been spent in and around New York City, but I cannot claim an intense feeling of identification with the city. In a sense, one is cheated by being born here. The newcomer never entirely recovers from his stunning first impression, while the native becomes aware of the city gradually and without a thrill of wonder. Very early, those of us raised in the outlying areas fall into the habit of saying we are "going to the city" when, in fact, we are already within its boundaries. By the city we mean, of course, Manhattan, as does everyone who speaks of New York. Yet there is another New York, unstoried and rather drab, consisting of provincial Brooklyn, Queens, and the Bronx. It lies only a subway ride away from Manhattan, and most of us make this journey for the whole of our working lives, but proximity does not foster a sense of belonging there.

Ours is a daylight, hurry-up, cash-and-carry relationship with Manhattan; our business completed, we are shot through underground tubes and dispersed. The people who sleep in Manhattan are mainly the rich and the poor. Eight out of ten of the middle and upper-middle income families in the New York metropolitan area live in the outlying parts of the city and the suburbs. These millions of people are the unnoticed New Yorkers, the blurred walk-ons who provide the human backdrop for Manhattan's vivid extremes of glamour and squalor. They come from places like Richmond Hill, a neighborhood in south Queens where three generations of my family have lived in tree-shaded frame houses on forty-foot lots. The people in Richmond Hill, and all the neighborhoods like it, are as much strangers to Harlem or Sutton Place as any tourist, yet they are New Yorkers, and the life of the city depends on their exertions. They do not live splendidly or squalidly; they merely try to live decently. The purpose of this essay is to explore some of the obstacles to achieving this modest objective in the world's greatest city.

The fashionably tough-minded myth persists that the world's greatest city owes its inhabitants nothing, except the chance to grab the brass ring. Out of a kind of sad, proud stoicism, New Yorkers cling to this lie to convince themselves they are still in the running when they know they are not. It is the only consolation prize New York offers. The truth is that the New Yorker of humble talents and ambitions derives no benefit from living in the world's greatest city, but instead pays more for less with each passing year. He would be better off living in Cleveland, where at least he would not have to pretend that second-rate is best. The glorious success that New York bestows on the few has been well advertised; we should not neglect the mute endurance and debased expectations it inflicts on the many.

I am not immune to the drama of the city, but it is best enjoyed from a comfortable seat; the view from the sidewalks is quite different. Nor do I undervalue the city's unique advantages; but I know that most of the ones that matter—I am not thinking of the Museum of Natural History—are available only to those who can afford them. New York is too often judged by its exceptional features, and excused for the mean quality (or total absence) of ordinary amenities. There are as many "private" New Yorks as the taste and imagination of individual New Yorkers can discover; I am interested in the "public" city that, to a greater or lesser degree, we all share. Whatever our private delights and successes, we find within this common physical environment tragic deprivation and massive failure.

People outside New York have no cause for smugness, particularly if they are among the seven out of ten Americans who live in and around cities. They may be spared the peculiar oppressiveness of living in New York, but they cannot escape the shadow that New York's failure throws across the future of an increasingly urban civilization.

Quite obviously, the mounting disorder of the nation's largest city is unique in the sense that its scope cannot be duplicated elsewhere. Every large U.S. city is different, and each will succeed or fail as an environment in its own terms. But the uniqueness of New York is not absolute. Although this world metropolis has seemed alien and unrepresentative to the rest of the country since the days when Squire Tom Jefferson denounced it as "a cloacina of all the depravities of human nature," New York is destroying itself under the impact of forces that are being felt in every city. New York represents the fullest expression—for good or ill—of our urban culture. It is the macrocosm of every city's problems and aspirations. It matters, therefore, to Americans everywhere what New York is—and what it is not.

2 New York is, of course, a miracle. Through an infinitely complex mechanism, millions of people are fed, housed, clothed, transported, and organized for work that, in turn, organizes the work of millions of other people throughout the nation and the world. On Manhattan Island is found the greatest concentration of human skill and energy in the world. Here is the economic, cultural, and intellectual capital of the Western world. Here is the headquarters of U.S. industry and the vital center of the economy. It is impossible to overestimate the power and magnetism of New York. But how fares the human spirit in this great metropolis?

New York's failure is in human arrangements, a failure with many sources. It can be traced to the apathy and venality of the city's politicians; to the cold unconcern of the city's builders, among whom a kind of Gresham's Law of architecture prevails; to the remoteness and indifference of the city's business and financial leaders; to the selfishness of competing groups and interests whose actions and demands take little account of the general welfare.

For several weeks during the summer of 1964, Fifth Avenue, being repaved for the first time in forty-one years, was a no-man's land of trenches and rubble, half closed off by barricades and dominated by mechanical shovels. Stalled buses herded together like captured elephants, throwing up clouds of stinking fumes. The rattling jackhammers and snorting compressors on Fifth merged with the din along Sixth. There, in the space of six blocks, three new giant buildings were rearing up, their scaffolding encroaching on the street. Work on a subway extension disrupted traffic, as it will until 1967. Construction and excavation claimed all but two lanes of the clogged avenue; machinery and materials spilled over mud-splattered temporary sidewalks. Assailed on all sides, impeded and frustrated at every turn, people pushed through the confusion.

Stirred to indignation rather belatedly, the New York Chapter of the American Institute of Architects in June, 1964, issued an unprecedented report on "The State of the City." The architects were appalled. They found alarming retrogession beneath the surface of the city's vaunted "progress," and concluded grimly that "New York City is not getting benefits commensurate with the money, energy, and effort that are going into its development. The uncoordinated development of the city, the growth of traffic problems, the continued pollution of air and water, the churning destruction and frantic rebuilding—all these are taking their toll."

New York is an economic entity; it exists primarily to perform work; to permit the ease of human contact that facilitates the exchange of goods and services. But the city functions today only with growing difficulty and inefficiency. Concentration is yielding to strangling congestion, energy is misdirected and therefore wasted, so that the disadvantages of the city are visibly outpacing the advantages. The economic costs of its malfunctioning have become staggering, as businessmen recognize. As Peter M. Stanford, a trustee of the City Club, has declared, "Business, large and small, has lost confidence in New York."

In terms of creating jobs, New York's economy is stagnant. During the five-year period from 1958 to 1963, non-farm employment across the nation increased by 11.1 percent, while New York's employment increased by only 1.6 percent. Outside of the construction industry and government bureaucracy, the city did not generate a single additional job in this five-year span, and even construction has declined recently. Instead, New York lost 76,000 jobs in its factory industries, thereby worsening the plight of its large unskilled and semiskilled work force. As it is, the average factory wage paid in New York is the lowest of any major American city.

However, it is not the economic disorder of New York that throws a shadow across an urban civilization. The truly terrible costs of New York are social and spiritual. These accrue

16

in endless human discomfort, inconvenience, harassment, and fear, which have become part of the pervasive background, like the noise and filth, but are much deadlier. For it is people who breathe life into an environment, who create and sustain the vitality of a healthy city. If people are driven and their senses dulled, if they are alienated and dehumanized, the city is on the way to destroying itself.

For the rich as well as the poor, some of the good things of life are unobtainable in New York. As Lewis Mumford has observed in *The Culture of Cities,* "the so-called blighted areas of the metropolis are essentially *'do without'* areas." In this sense, much of New York outside the slums is "blighted," and the people living there, as Mumford has written, are "people who do without pure air, who do without sound sleep, who do without a cheerful garden or playing space, who do without the very sight of the sky and the sunlight, who do without free motion, spontaneous play . . ." Among those imprisoned within such an environment, he writes, "chronic starvation produces lack of appetite. Eventually, you may live and die without even recognizing the loss."

3 New York shows alarming signs of spiritual malnutrition and death-by-inches. It is frowning, tight-lipped, short-tempered, the most nervous city in America. It is a city without grace. It is humorless, able to mock and taunt, but too tense to gain the release of laughter. It is a city that cries "Jump" to a would-be suicide perched on a window ledge.

The city itself sways on the edge of madness. It almost plunged over during the summer of 1964, when Negro mobs surged through Harlem and the Bedford-Stuyvesant section of Brooklyn, rioting and looting, while sweating, cursing white policemen wearing steel helmets fired volleys of shots in the air. The floodlights and leaping flames in the streets exposed frightening realities: the state of war existing between Negroes and police; the inability of so-called Negro leaders to control or even communicate with their presumed followers; the immeasurably greater failure of white political and civic leaders who possess power, but who lack the will and imagination to use it. The riots were produced not by Negro militancy, but by alienation and hopelessness in the ghettos, and apathy in the city at large.

Perhaps the saddest feature of the riots was the presence of mere children in the mobs, many of them barely in their teens yet already filled with contempt for "Whitey's" law. Some of the reasons for such behavior are not hard to discover. More than 50 percent of Harlem's children live with neither or only one of their parents. The delinquency rate is 115.8 per thou-

sand in central Harlem, compared with 50.6 per thousand in the city as a whole. The median family income in Harlem is $3,500 annually, compared with $5,100 for the white population of the city. Nearly 50 percent of Harlem's housing is officially classified as deteriorated or dilapidated. The infant mortality rate in the ghetto is twice that of the city as a whole.

A year after the riots, much talk and increased public spending (most of it siphoned off by the politically favored), have left untouched the chaotic social conditions within the ghettos. While the political generals in the much-ballyhooed "War on Poverty" quarrel among themselves, the people sit blank-eyed on tenement stoops and the wild, unwanted children aimlessly loiter in schoolyards and on street corners. The police still walk their beats under the sullen gaze of their enemies, aware that an arrest is likely to bring an encircling mob into the streets in a matter of seconds. Nothing has changed because the indifference of the powerful is inherent in the very existence of Harlem and Bedford-Stuyvesant.

Whether or not the city suffers further racial explosions, it will remain frightened by its inner turmoil and capacity for violence. Anyone searching for the causes of New York's decline encounters problems of awesome complexity, but a fundamental cause is starkly apparent and simply expressed: *the city is not safe.* In any city, someone who goes looking for trouble will usually find it; in New York, the most prudent citizen runs the risk of falling victim to sudden, often senseless violence. Indeed, the distinctive characteristic of crime in New York may be its random, unprovoked savagery. On an evening in May, an elderly woman, standing on a subway platform in Queens, is accosted by a twelve-year-old girl she has never seen before, who wordlessly stabs her to death. Later that night, at the World's Fair, a fourteen-year-old fatally knifes a twenty-year-old stranger following an argument over a nickel.

City newspapers long ago gave up headlining crime "waves," perhaps because there are no longer any troughs of comparative calm. What has been happening in New York is more like the relentless rise of flood waters. No crest is in sight, and the wall of order protecting society cannot hold indefinitely. From 1963 to 1964, major crimes of violence in New York increased 13 percent. Murder rose 16 percent, forcible rape 28 percent, robbery 17 percent. On the transit system, serious crimes increased during the year by 52 percent, a figure so startling that Mayor Robert F. Wagner took the extreme and costly but popular step of ordering a police guard on every subway train and station during the nighttime hours.

Such posting of sentries is the sort of precaution civilized outsiders take when they venture into a hostile wilderness. Is the world's greatest city no safer than a jungle? Certainly, to the extent that New Yorkers feel endangered in their ordinary pursuits, they have been reduced to the status of outsiders in their own city. The law-abiding are unarmed by law, but lack confidence that there are enough law enforcement officers to protect them. On upper Park Avenue, frightened apartment dwellers have dressed their doormen in police uniforms. In some poorer neighborhoods, usually after particularly atrocious crimes, panic-stricken citizens have acknowledged the reality of the jungle and banded together to form vigilance committees which patrol the streets after dark.

Only when the encroachments of the jungle are considered in sum does one realize how they narrow the margin of civilized existence in New York. It is a small thing, surely, for a young mother living in an apartment house in a "good" neighborhood not to be able to go unescorted to the basement laundry room. It is no catastrophe that an elderly man chooses to go without tobacco rather than walk to the corner shop on a poorly lighted street. Those women who work at night and those who wish to cast off loneliness by visiting friends or going to a movie, can, if they are afraid to ride the subway, take taxicabs at additional expense. And they can stay at home if they are afraid of unguarded lobbies and self-service elevators. In broad daylight, mothers and children can use the city's green spaces, such as Washington Square in Greenwich Village, only apprehensively, because derelicts, sex perverts, and hoodlums congregate there. Of course, they can stay at home. That alternative is always available to the weak and defenseless in New York: stay at home. Thus, many who tolerate and sacrifice much to live in the city are, in one way or another, denied the use and enjoyment of the city. During

23

the civil rights march in Alabama last spring, in which city officials ostentatiously participated, a New Yorker wrote plaintively to the Herald Tribune: *"We also need a great civil rights march in our city to insure to us the civil rights to live in our homes, to ride in our subways, to walk in our streets and parks at any hour without fear of being murdered, robbed and raped." In this city of double-locked doors, where two-legged predators strut and law-abiding citizens are afraid, it is time we asked: Who are the jailed and who are the jailors?*

4 In New York, the voices of special interest are never still, while the voice of common interest is seldom raised. Perhaps the great mass of New Yorkers are not so much apathetic as they are accustomed to being ignored or dealt with as statistics, which is the same thing. They resignedly learn to tolerate the intolerable. It may be impossible to mobilize their submerged civic concern and pride on behalf of the entire community, but we cannot find out if no one attempts the task of leading the unorganized majority.

An ideal "issue" on which to make the attempt is air pollution, which is universally deplored and potentially the concern of everyone who draws breath. The foul air of New York, dirtier than that of any other major city, threatens public health and costs the citizens an estimated $520 million annually. Our dirty atmosphere is intolerable and could be cleansed by the enforcement of stringent laws. Yet we go on tolerating it. Nothing more neatly underscores the pathetic deprivations of city life than the fact that private citizens, alarmed at official neglect of an essential public interest, found it necessary to organize a pressure group, Citizens for Clean Air, Inc. Soon afterward, a special committee of the City Council, headed by the able Councilman Robert A. Low, launched a study of air pollution. Its interim findings, released this summer, remind us that we are poisoning ourselves with every breath we take.

"It has been generally concluded," reports the Low Committee, "that air pollution is one of the factors contributing to the steady increase of lung cancer." A person breathing the city's air inhales as much benzpyrene, a cancer-inducing hydrocarbon, as he would if he smoked two packs of cigarettes a day. Dust particles can carry the benzpyrene to sensitive areas of the lungs—and there is no lack of dust in the city. On every square mile of New York, an average of 60 tons of heavy dust falls each month; in Manhattan, 80 tons. This is the filth that begrimes shirt collars and blackens windows; the deadly pollutants are the ones we cannot see—chiefly carbon monoxide, nitrogen dioxide, and sulfur dioxide. The average level and the maximum level of sulfur dioxide recorded in New York are higher than in any other major U.S. city.

While the menace of air pollution to public health is plain, medical researchers, poring over statistical studies of the city's recurring smog episodes, are compelled to speak only of "excess deaths," mainly among infants and elderly persons. Some 170 "excess deaths" occurred in November, 1953, when a nine-day "temperature inversion" caused pollutants to accumulate in the air over the city. During a two-week period in early 1963, a combination of heavy air pollution, extreme cold, and an epidemic of Asian influenza is believed to have caused some 400 more deaths than normal in New York. If hundreds of people fell dead on the streets, action would come at once. But the figures on "excess deaths" come to public attention at the measured pace of scientific research, long after the fact, and so lose much of their impact. A do-nothing Mayor greets such figures with a statement piously cautioning against "incitement to fright and panic."

Observes a researcher who studies New York's atmosphere: "Air pollution exemplifies what happens in a chaotic situation. Everyone's lack of concern mixes in the air."

To provide the people with tolerably clean air is a prime responsibility of municipal government. But that huge, self-frustrating entity, which officially opposes air pollution, also contributes mightily to it. Indeed, what the city negligently does to worsen air pollution, such as operating a fleet of 4,200 poorly maintained buses, makes a mockery of its official opposition. The city's Department of Air Pollution Control is a stepchild agency, with a budget of just over a million dollars a year, and an enforcement staff of only forty-five inspectors to cover 320 square miles. Ironically, much of the soot the city chases comes, as the result of official expediency, from 12,000 apartment-house incinerators. In 1951 the Department of Sanitation, short of trucks and dumping grounds, lobbied through a municipal regulation requiring incinerators in new apartment houses four stories or higher. Burning garbage in an inefficient apartment-house incinerator reduces its bulk by as little as 25 percent, an accommodation to the Sanitation Department for which New Yorkers pay a fantastic price. New York's uniquely bad sulfur dioxide pollution is the result of the city's complacently allowing large fuel oil users, such as factories, apartment houses, and Con Edison power plants (Con Edison is the largest user of all, burning half the city's fuel), to burn a cheap, sludgy grade of oil with a high sulfur content. Over the next few years, under a new fuel oil code, such users will have to substitute a somewhat better and "cleaner" grade of oil.

Thus does New York attack enormous problems with toothpicks. Arthur J. Benline, Commissioner of Air Pollution Control, has perfectly expressed the prevailing official attitude: "The best we can do now is to conduct a holding action, hoping that we can keep things from getting worse."

Few tidily isolated problems exist in New York; one problem interacts with and compounds another. Thus, the 600,000 automobiles that enter Manhattan's central business district

27

each day not only intensify air pollution, but also snarl traffic and encourage grossly inefficient allocation of public funds. Each of these cars carries an average of one and a half persons, hardly a fair exchange for the nuisance it creates. The city Highways Department and the Port of New York Authority cannot build and expand access roads fast enough to keep up with the traffic congestion that roads are creating. Meanwhile, mass transportation is neglected.

No one can estimate the time and energy consumed in merely trying to move people and goods about the streets of New York. Up and down the blocks off Seventh Avenue between Thirty-fifth and Fortieth Streets, parking is forbidden by city traffic regulations, but "standing" while making a delivery is not. Trucks line every foot of curb and remain "standing" for hours. One even occupies the restricted zone in front of a fire house. Without such wholesale mockery of ineffective parking regulations, the city's garment industry— the largest factory industry in New York—could not survive. Even so, the number of workers in the needle trades has steadily dwindled (by more than 30,000 between 1958 and 1963), partly because small employers cannot bear the cost of fighting city traffic. On Thirty-sixth Street, a policeman, his shirt stained black from perspiration, extricates a large trailer truck from the tangle of the street—it is blocking traffic for the length of the block—and guides the driver as he backs into what will clearly be a parking space, but what the hope-

lessly overwhelmed enforcers of law prefer to see as a "standing" space. Whatever it may be called, the misuse of streets as loading terminals and parking (and double-parking) *lots is strangling the city.*

No less mortal is the misuse of Manhattan's limited land as a right-of-way for through traffic, as though nothing—not homes or businesses or jobs or the permanent blighting effects of a highway—were as important as vehicular convenience. The long-proposed Lower Manhattan Expressway would remove through truck traffic from a mile and a half of congested local streets between the Holland Tunnel from New Jersey and the Williamsburg and Manhattan bridges to Brooklyn. But the elevated, eight-lane highway also would cut a deadly swath 160 feet wide—more than three-quarters of a Manhattan block—through a neighborhood, uprooting 2,000 families, forcing 800 businesses to relocate, and wiping out as many as 12,000 jobs. The loss of these jobs, now held chiefly by Negroes and Puerto Ricans, would be especially hurtful to the city. (When an opponent of the expressway pointed out that the jobs it would destroy are held mainly by workers who have difficulty finding employment, a leading union official replied coldly: "I can't be worried about them.") Those who remained in the area would be confronted daily by the massive, overshadowing pillars of the expressway dividing their neighborhood. (Oddly enough, the city that plans to erect this structure spent millions of dollars not many years ago tearing down the dark els on Third and Sixth Avenues, which was a major factor in reviving these rundown streets.)

On official maps this already appears as a "blighted" area. And so it is, in large measure because the expressway route has been mapped on the city's "master plan" since 1941, and the phantom highway has forced the area to exist in a limbo. Owners cannot obtain loans to repair and improve buildings that lie in the path of the bulldozer. Businesses that might have remained move away. The neighborhood declines as people who can afford other living quarters flee uncertainty and the tender mercies of the city bureaucracy. Consider this official advice from the Department of Real Estate on how to transplant people: Persons "who have physical or mental disability which hinder relocation should be referred to the social worker . . . Often, mental retardation may be identified if a person gives confused, vague, conflicting or irrelevant responses to the Relocation Manager's initial interview for Site Occupant Record card data. Very often, a problem case may be identified as an individual or family who seems unable to comprehend the necessity for relocation."

For a time, it seemed that residents of the neighborhood and allies throughout the city had succeeded in halting the project, but Mayor Wagner, after much backing and filling, finally has given it the green light. City officials, union leaders, and businessmen are pleased. On paper, the $110 million expressway will cost the city nothing: the federal government will pay

90 percent, the state 10 percent. With unemployment in the construction industry now approaching 15 percent, the project means steady jobs for thousands of workers for two or three years. It is difficult to see why, if the highway must be built, it cannot follow a loop route around Manhattan, bypassing the central city as interstate traffic should. The more modest proposal of the Regional Plan Association that the expresssway be built below ground level to ease its blighting effects has been brushed aside as impractical, even though the city has built depressed highways in other areas where the advantages are less obvious. Apparently, the easiest way to build a road is to draw a line on a map and then push the people out of the way.

Space literally does not exist for an ever increasing number of trucks and automobiles in Manhattan, yet the city's ingenious traffic planners continually strive to make room on the island for the traffic their plans stimulate. Sometimes their proposal is to lop off a few feet of sidewalk here and there, in the apparent conviction that machinery enjoys a higher claim to space than people. Sometimes the planners propose to make "practical" use of parks, such as excavating part of Madison Square Park and shoving a 780-car garage underneath it, at a cost of about $6,000 per parking space. A grandiose plan calls for building seven parking garages in congested midtown at a cost of $35 million. Even if Manhattan were paved over —35.5 percent of its total land area is already taken up by streets, highways, and expressways—the automobile would remain insatiable. Either we will tame it, severely restricting its use within the city while simultaneously improving mass transportation; or the automobile will inexorably devour what remains of human living space in the city.

Were it not for some natural advantages, which offset human neglect and waste, the predicament of New York would be considerably worse. For example, the prevailing westerly winds above the city, while they carry industrial fumes over from New Jersey, blow much of the air pollution out to sea. Nature also bestowed her bounty on the city in the form of a magnificent deepwater harbor, broad rivers, and a network of bays and inlets—a bounty that New York has squandered through carelessness, and may have diminished irretrievably.

First, let us try to find the water. The city's waterfront is longer than the canals of Venice, but one does not think of Manhattan as an island, even within a block or two of the water's edge. For the city has walled itself in. Highways separate the inhabitants from the water, and tall buildings rise above the roads, shutting out the view of the rivers. (These structures are built on so-called "air rights," which, if they belong to anyone, are the property of the people of New York.) If pedestrians want to enjoy the river view, they must traverse bridges above the traffic flow and use fenced, isolated paths perfectly suited for muggings and other crimes.

The waters around New York are heavily polluted, the result of the shortsighted assumption over several generations that, regardless of what the city heedlessly did, it could not destroy so great a natural asset. The cumulative effect of popular and political indifference has been felt in recent generations. It was cheaper to lay one pipe to carry both sewage and storm water rather than two, so the city built combined sewers, which overflow treatment plants following even a moderate rainfall. As recently as 1935 the city did not have a single modern treatment plant, and it still does not have enough of them. It routinely pumps raw sewage into the Hudson and East rivers, more than a half billion gallons daily, relying on what sanitary engineers vividly describe as "excellent flushes." As a result of such disgusting "flushing" along much of the 150-mile course from Albany to New York, the mighty Hudson, "the great river of the mountains," has become a rank cesspool. According to state studies, the river is six times more polluted than it was at the turn of the century while the state's population has increased less than two and a half times. The despoliation by preceding generations denies ourselves and our children (and probably *their* children) a significant part of our natural heritage. Even if all forms of pollution were magically to cease tomorrow, the befouled Hudson could not cleanse itself, and be fit for swimming and fishing, until well into the next century. The end of pollution is not in sight, of course, but the city experienced a painful retribution for its profligacy during the dry summer of 1965. With its upstate reservoirs dangerously low, and a water emergency declared, the city

35

was forced to begin planning the costly and time-consuming chlorination of the same river water it pollutes. Water, water everywhere . . .

5 And what of the land? Of America's large cities, San Francisco is commonly considered to be the one most pleasing to the eye. The majestic sweep of the bay engages the viewer; his pleasure grows as his eye examines streets and buildings near at hand. Steep as its hills are, it is a city for walking. In some respects the natural endowments of New York are richer than those of San Francisco. Indeed New York is a dramatic spectacle from unusual perspectives: from a plane or a tall building, from the deck of an ocean liner coming up the harbor. At nightfall, as lighted office windows hang suspended in the dusk like a string of lanterns stretching across the sky, the scene is breathtaking. As the viewer enters the streets, however, the drama abruptly dissolves, for the city has risen up on an inhuman scale.

The explanation usually given is obvious, and unsatisfying: shortage of space on the island has caused high land prices (as much as $400 a square foot), which in turn necessitate high densities. But is it necessary for compactness to be so ugly? Compactness could become a virtue if builders cared about

36

the appearance of what they built. The increasing ugliness of the city's streets was not foreordained; men are making New York the eyesore so much of it is.

The word "eyesore" calls to mind ramshackle tenements—slums—and New York has them: about 15 per cent of its 2.8 million dwelling units are in some stage of disrepair. A slum is a place where poor people all too visibly live. Builders in New York have contrived to erect miles of apartment houses in which no one appears to live, monotonous cubes and ominous towers, which repel the eye with their harsh angularity and dreary sameness. Tiers of whirring air conditioners are the only evidence that these sterile-looking buildings are inhabited.

In Manhattan's business districts, the same lifeless architecture prevails, with occasional stunning exceptions. Construction has long been considered synonymous with "progress," and myth-makers tell us that frenzied demolition and rebuilding somehow express the "spirit" of New York, its restless energy and passion for novelty. This mystique may bemuse the tourist and foreign journalist, who are primed to appreciate what the Mayor is pleased to call "the throbbing vitality" of the metropolis. The resident knows better. All too often, the wrecker's ball crashes and the bulldozer ravages for no better reason than to enable someone to make a quick buck.

In their report on the city, the architects declared that "the field of speculative and investment architecture requires much more serious consideration than it has received heretofore." Pointing out what had long been obvious, they noted that buildings "erected for the sole purpose of income or a quick profit . . . deeply affect present and future dollar values, community desirability, the rate of urban decay and obsolescence, the city's attractiveness and inspiration for residents and its appeal to tourists."

The driving force of New York's construction boom has been the need to house a rapidly expanding office work force. Office buildings in the central business district occupy only 1.7 percent of the city's total acreage, but they provide more than one million jobs—fully half of the city's total employment. From 1946 through the end of 1964, a total of 64 million square feet of office space was built in Manhattan. This represents more space than was built in the central business districts of the next twenty-two largest urban areas in the country combined. With a handful of exceptions, the buildings are the standardized product of builders who are strictly in the business of manufacturing space.

The City Planning Commission has described Manhattan as "the most preferred real-estate location in the world"—so choice, apparently, that planning officials are not allowed to trespass on it. The real power lies in hands holding private purse strings. Through their collective decisions, the speculative builders and, even more important, the mortgage lenders in the banks and insurance companies have reshaped the

contours of New York, determining how the city functions and how its inhabitants live. Provided with incentives by every level of government, these private decision makers of great public power have feverishly torn down, rebuilt, and expanded, profitably manipulating the land beneath buildings and even the air above. In the process they have established the rule that in New York the land and the buildings define the place of people. People are regarded not as human beings but as economic units. Even in the aggregate, their wishes are outweighed by columns of figures.

Not long before his death, Vincent Astor wished to raise a monument to himself in the form of a slim tower of offices and a block-long plaza on Park Avenue. Combined with the open space in front of the handsome Seagram Building across the street, this would have created a pleasant promenade in crowded midtown, a place to stroll, similar to Rockefeller Center. But Astor was unable to find financing. His idea may not have been too sound but this is not the point. The point is that the very sound First National City Bank took over the site, and erected a bulky building covering every square foot.

According to Carl A. Morse, president of the Diesel Construction Co., Inc., builder of the Pan Am Building and other major office structures, "the difference in cost between an aesthetically pleasing building and an ordinary one is nominal, since structurally and mechanically most buildings are or should be pretty nearly equal." In a $15 million office building, Morse estimates, "1 to 2 percent additional is all that is required to give a feeling of quality."

Although it is doubtful that true quality architecture can be obtained quite so economically there are corporate sponsors willing to pay a premium for a distinctive building. Unhappily, the tax-hungry city seems determined to discourage them. Precisely because the Seagram Building departs from the practice of squeezing every square foot of rentable space from a site, and instead sits gracefully behind a half-acre plaza and lovely pools and fountains which the public enjoys, the building has been treated as a special case by the real-estate tax assessor. Its valuation has been calculated, not on the usual basis of rental income, but on the basis of replacement cost. As a result, the assessment on the building has been hiked from $19 million to $26 million, which adds $400,000 to the annual tax bill. In effect, Seagram has been punished for daring to raise a distinguished building among mediocre ones, a precedent likely to deter others who aspire to architectural excellence.

Fashions change in New York speculative building. The famous soaring towers that dominate the city's skyline date from the boom of the nineteen-twenties. The typical office building constructed during the post-World War II boom is squat and bulky. It rises plumb with the building line, with setbacks occurring at intervals determined not by aesthetic considerations but to beat the restrictions of the zoning code.

44

This ziggurat style of skyscraper has but one purpose: to maximize the builder's profit. There is nothing wrong in principle with maximizing profits, which are the motivating force of progress. What is wrong is the rules under which builders are allowed to operate.

Let us suppose a builder plans to erect a building that will cost $6 million, $1 million representing the land and $5 million the building. In theory, he can obtain mortgage financing for only two-thirds of that amount, or $4 million. Actually, he will have little difficulty obtaining considerably more, but for the sake of illustration figure his equity at $2 million. Though his equity is only $2 million (or less), the New York builder can depreciate the entire $5 million cost of the building at an accelerated rate, getting $250,000 in tax-free cash flow back the first year. Even if rental income falls short of expectations, the builder enjoys a comfortable cushion. The speculative builder usually expects to get his money back in seven years. When he has used up his depreciation he may sell the building to a syndicate at an inflated price, which becomes the basis for another profitable ride aboard the accelerated-depreciation gimmick. In the eyes of its owners, the building that will loom above the city streets for twenty years or more is only an entry in an accountant's ledger; the structure is less important as a building than as a tax shelter.

Because of the tax laws uniquely favoring speculative building and real-estate syndication, an experienced and unusually candid operator denies that his ventures involve capitalism. "It's state socialism for the rich."

An example of such "socialism" is federally subsidized urban renewal, which enables the favored real-estate operator to enrich himself through the use of municipal power. Property condemned by the city under its power of eminent domain is turned over to the developer at a bargain price; he also may receive city and state government incentives in the form of liberal financing and tax abatement. All he must do is build decent, low-cost housing. In some instances, however, urban-renewal sponsors in New York have taken over slum properties from the city at bargain prices—and then have continued to collect rents for months and even years without turning a spade of dirt. The city Housing Authority itself, pressed to find accommodations for low-income families displaced by renewal projects and unable to get into public housing, owns and operates forty tenements, some of them as rundown as the city's worst slum buildings.

Jane Jacobs, author of the brilliant *Death and Life of Great American Cities,* which demolished a host of city planning myths, believes that New York's first zoning code in 1916 opened up endless possibilities for the use of government power for private gain. "It introduced the idea of recasting areas of the city by government action. The big prize became getting the government to do what you wanted it to do. Government and the actions of government became the means of making great fortunes."

Zoning remains the instrument usually relied upon to protect the public interest and improve the city's physical environment. Largely because so many obviously tawdry buildings were being erected amidst rising complaints, the original New York City zoning code was rewritten in 1960. However, before the new code took effect, the opposing real-estate and construction interests forced a concession: buildings for which plans were filed before December, 1961, could be erected under the old and more lenient code. Applications came in a torrent. "The zoning boom is a lasting tribute to the shortsightedness of some real-estate interests," William F. R. Ballard, chairman of the City Planning Commission, has declared. "In the rush to get in under the wire of the 1961 cutoff date, applications were filed for a colossal 150,659 multiple-dwelling units. That represented about five years' worth of housing."

The immediate effect of the new zoning code, therefore, was greatly to stimulate construction of the kind of building it was intended to discourage. It is hoped, rather forlornly, that the desired improvements—reduction in bulk, more openness of design, improved land use—will be apparent within a decade. More realistic is the expectation that the builders before long will be demanding "liberalization" of the code—that is, a return to the old one. Declares an official of the Planning Commission: "The builders will argue that new construction is off. Which it is. But it is only because there was so much wild *over*building."

The new code was aimed at the ziggurat skyscraper; in its place is emerging a style that, at least in theory, is aesthetically satisfying—a tower rising from a block base. But the change is more apparent than real. Provided a builder assembles a large enough site and leaves open space at street level for a plaza effect, he may, if he pleases, consider the sky the limit, building vertically to gain *more* square feet of rentable space than would have been possible on the same site under the old code. "All the new code does is eliminate the small man," explains a knowing builder. "If you have less than 10,000 square feet to build on, it's now impossible."

6 The new megalith style of skyscraper is exemplified by the Pan Am Building, the world's largest commercial office building, which hulks brutally over Grand Central Terminal. This fifty-nine-story octagonal tower, which houses 25,000 workers, was wedged into one of the most congested areas of the city. Significantly, although it was built under the old zoning code, it could have been erected under the new one as well. Harassed city planners used this eloquent fact to clear themselves of the charge that they were seeking *too much* *power*. The Planning Commission, which nominally oversees the city's physical environment, was powerless to influence the construction of the Pan Am Building. It did not even bother to study the traffic problems likely to be created, because, as a city planner admits somewhat abashedly, "it wouldn't have made any difference *what* the study showed."

When the late Erwin Wolfson, who conceived the project, took account of the criticisms of the Pan Am Building, he found one with obvious merit. It was that no building should occupy the three-and-a-half acre site; that it should be an open plaza. "You have to agree with that," said Wolfson, adding almost wistfully: "It would be nice if it were possible." Of course, it was not; the land rights for the site were too valuable.

The only real restraint operating on Wolfson was self-imposed. Insisting that he was not immune to aesthetic and sociological considerations, he once pointed out that he could legally have constructed a five-million-square-foot monstrosity, which would have dumped into the Grand Central area twice as many workers as the Pan Am Building now does. With municipal agencies powerless to protect their interests, New Yorkers are forced to rely on such small mercies.

The interests behind the Pan Am Building regard it as entirely successful. The New York Central Railroad, which owns the land, will receive $1,100,000 annually over a seventy-seven-year lease. The building is now 99 percent occupied; Pan Am's lease alone calls for payment of $117 million over an unspecified term in excess of twenty-five years. The mortgage holders are pleased with their $66 million investment in a conspicuous "prestige" structure. The only interest that cannot be expressed in economic terms is that of the people.

Architects and urban designers, in their helpless fury, tended to overdraw the horrors the Pan Am Building would inflict on crowded Grand Central. During the year and a half of construction the noise was often deafening, but New York is perhaps the noisiest city in the world and none of the 500,000 benumbed human beings who passed through the terminal daily raised a protest.

Traffic still moves. The thousands of workers have been absorbed in the morning and nightly flood of subway riders. The noontime scramble for lunch-counter space is more frantic, but somehow the mob gulps hamburgers in fifteen-minute shifts. The sidewalks are packed, but not quite impassable. All that has happened, really, is that life has become more unpleasant for countless people. The critics were not wrong to attack the Pan Am Building as an architectural and sociological atrocity; they simply underestimated the capacity of New Yorkers to endure inhuman pressures.

And what, after all, is a vista worth? Can a citizen who once derived pleasure from the tracery of the old New York Central tower against the sky sue someone for the loss he suffers because the south end of Park Avenue is walled up? The signs he is now forced to view have commercial value, as

Pan American fully realized. The airline originally wanted signs thirty feet high on all eight sides of the building; it settled reluctantly for two smaller signs and a pair of company emblems.

In a certain sense, the signs and emblems are appropriate. A victorious force cannot be denied the ancient right to display its standard over conquered territory. Up and down Park Avenue, long synonymous with elegance, the glass curtain walls of new office buildings reflect the triumph of unalloyed commercialism. This change in character was inevitable once the thoroughfare caught the fancy of the mortgage lenders who wield decisive economic power. (Twenty-one banking offices are to be found along the avenue between Grand Central and Fifty-ninth Street.) Most of the glass buildings have a look of calculated (not to say, transparent) impermanence, as though they could be collapsed overnight on a tax lawyer's advice, but they possess a clear advantage over the stone buildings they are replacing: they are more profitable. The jet airplane has introduced travel habits which have made many midtown hotels uneconomic relics. This summer, the Park Lane Hotel at Forty-ninth Street is coming down to make way for an office building. There are a few solid-looking holdouts, such as the refurbished Waldorf-Astoria, but the attractiveness of Park Avenue is unmistakably fading, and only the contrasting dirt and clutter of the surrounding streets keep alive the illusion of elegance. Within a decade, Park Avenue seems destined to appear as coldly functional as Central Filing. Along its length, as in a gallery of mirrors, a society ruled by commercial values will catch hurried glimpses of its uninspiring image.

Perhaps thinking of what has been happening to Park Avenue—he did not specify—the distinguished architect Edward Durell Stone recently rendered a severe judgment. "Everything betrays us as a bunch of catchpenny materialists devoted to a blatant, screeching insistence on commercialism," he declared. "If you look around you, and you give a damn, it makes you want to commit suicide."

Embarrassingly enough, within weeks of this forceful pronouncement, architectural students were marching to protest the construction of a building of which Stone is co-architect. This is the giant General Motors Building, to be erected on the site of the unprofitable Savoy Plaza Hotel at Fifth Avenue and Fifty-ninth Street. It was no ordinary threat to urban amenity that moved the students to picket in a driving rain, but the prospect of a shocking violation of a cherished corner of the city. Around the small park and fountains on Fifth Avenue at Fifty-ninth Street are clustered shops and buildings which, though relatively undistinguished individually, unite to form an unusually harmonious environment, a graceful setting of repose and sophistication attractive to pedestrians. The Savoy Plaza on the east and the Plaza Hotel on the west guard this enclave. Now the wall was to be breached by a towering in-

truder, and the students waved placards reading "Shame!"

No shame attaches to Stone's professional involvement in this $60 million to $80 million project; his skill will improve the G.M. Building. The fact remains that construction of this building represents, not an improvement, but the destructive exploitation of the site. In order to get maximum rentable area under the new zoning code, the building will rise fifty stories and contain more than 1,500,000 square feet of office space. A plaza and gardens are provided in a courtyard below street level; however, these amenities will be reduced to triviality by the tower's overwhelming bulk. The building is twice as large as it would have to be if G.M. were the only tenant. G.M. owns only 50 percent and London Merchant Securities Ltd., a syndicate of British investors, owns the other half. The world's richest corporation, which could well afford its own "prestige" building, scaled to its own needs and the requirements of the site, prudently chooses to play by the prevailing rules that reward speculative bulk. As a result, the addition of the G.M. Building will diminish its surroundings, destroying the very charm that drew the corporation there. Not without a touch of sadness, Stone gives the nearby Plaza Hotel no more than another decade before it, too, will be pulled down by the compelling logic of real-estate economics.

The Plaza has bravely run ads promising to stand fast, but the headline—"The Day New York Disappeared"—sounds an ominously prophetic note. What can be done to prevent

New York from "disappearing" piecemeal? Joseph Watterson, editor of the *Journal of the American Institute of Architects,* has endorsed this proposal: "Within certain areas—all the downtown portion of the city, at least—no building permit should be issued until the owner and the architect of the property involved have appeared with their designs before a responsible commission and convinced them that the proposed building would be an asset to and an enhancement of its environment, not just economically, but visually. New York, and all cities, have taken too many steps backward because any building newer than the one it replaced was considered better. It is inescapable that old buildings must be torn down, sometimes. But it is inexcusable that what replaces them should be poorer architecture. If a new building is not better in every way than the one it is replacing, it has no justification whatever."

7 New York exists only in the present tense. Just as there is no sense of obligation to the future, so there is no feeling of pride in the past. Although Manhattan is quite old—it was first settled in 1615—it is, as Alexander Woollcott once remarked, "a town without any attics." The city seems to regard the past with contempt and

hastens to obliterate its heritage. Even allowing for losses due to natural hazards such as fires, the near-totality of devastation is remarkable. This three-hundred-year-old city does not contain a single seventeenth-century building; only one pre-Revolutionary structure of architectural significance still exists; and only eight buildings in all of Manhattan date to the eighteenth century.

After several years of agitation by persistent citizens against the determined opposition of real-estate and business interests, the city recently enacted a landmarks preservation law. Based on the example and experience of some seventy-five other cities, the law is believed to be the most comprehensive in the country. It establishes a permanent Landmarks Preservation Commission, composed of at least three architects, a city planner or landscape architect, an architectural historian, and a representative of the city's real-estate interests. Under the law, a building designated as a landmark must be at least thirty years old and possess historical or architectural merit. So far, the commission has identified some seven hundred structures throughout the city as worthy of preservation. Should the owner of a designated landmark propose to demolish it, the commission is granted time to devise a plan to preserve the building. (Acting on the commonsense belief that not every landmark can be turned into a museum, a committee of architects is inventing new uses for old buildings—e.g., the Prospect Park boathouse would be converted into a restaurant, with outdoor tables.) Whatever plan the commission comes up with would assure the owner a reasonably profitable return—at least 6 percent of the structure's assessed valuation, plus 2 percent for depreciation—through a realty tax remission or exemption.

Opposing the measure, on the ground that it infringed on property owners' rights and interests, were the Real Estate Board of New York, the Commerce and Industry Association of New York, the Downtown-Lower Manhattan Association, and the Avenue of the Americas Association—an imposing cross-section of the city's business community. Businessmen generally agree with the principle of preservation, so long as it does not interfere with their right to do as they please with their property; which is to say that they oppose preservation in practice. A spokesman for the owners' division of the Real Estate Board, arguing that the law would "seriously impede the modern expansion and progress of the city," suggested, in all seriousness, that commemorative plaques would adequately preserve historic landmarks.

Mayor Wagner, to his credit, resisted the pressures on him to veto the bill, but in a final revision a loophole was introduced which, combined with the hostility of powerful interests, could defeat the purpose of the new law. After an initial period of eighteen months during which landmarks are to be designated, the commission will be allowed to select buildings or districts for protection only once every three years. The rest of the time the wreckers will be free to ply their trade as usual. The ruthless rebuilding of New York has already gone so far that the city soon could find itself, as the New York *Times* has warned, with "an excellent protective law and almost nothing to protect."

Symbolic of New York's self-destructive frenzy is the demolition of Pennsylvania Station, now being razed to make way for a $120-million complex including a new Madison Square Garden arena, an exhibition hall, bowling alleys, and a thirty-three-story office tower. This will be the fourth Madison Square Garden in eighty-five years. There will never be another Penn Station.

The terminal, designed by Charles Follen McKim and opened in 1910, was frankly imitative, derived from the ancient Roman Baths of Caracalla. Penn Station was not especially old, nor could it honestly be called a great work of architecture. It was black with soot, the interior was despoiled by garish billboards, and the roof leaked in winter. The terminal reportedly was operating at a $2,500,000-a-year loss. Therefore, the Pennsylvania Railroad decided to get rid of it. The Pennsy had been thinking of building an office building over the station, but when it learned that Irving Felt, president of the Graham-Paige Investment Co., was seeking a site for a new Madison Square Garden, it approached him. Attracted by the prospect of acquiring a square block in one deal, Felt struck a bargain with the Pennsy. The railroad is a one-fourth partner in the Madison Square Garden Corp., and will receive about $1 million a year in rental for the air rights over the new terminal.

So why not tear Penn Station down? Because that same soaring roof of steel and glass once enclosed the most impressive public space in the city. Penn Station had gained distinction through usage; it was a well-defined *place* in a city becoming featureless. Is it sentimental to treasure a building designed when men had a more considerable estimate of themselves? For a half century, travelers arriving in the world's greatest city entered through a suitable portal. They soon will enter through what amounts to a subway station. The portal through which many now enter is Kennedy International Airport—set in the marshes of Jamaica Bay, an hour's dreary, $6 to $7 cab ride away from Manhattan. Nor was Penn Station a hopeless anachronism in the jet age. One day the high-speed (over 200 miles per hour) intercity trains now being discussed will be a reality, rejuvenating rail passenger service between New York and Washington and Chicago; but New York's old, spacious terminal will be gone.

A group of architects organized themselves as the Action Group for Better Architecture (AGBANY) and fought the Madison Square Garden project before the City Planning Commission. The then chairman, James Felt, disqualified himself from ruling on his brother Irving's cause, but the issue had been decided by the amount of money involved. When an

AGBANY spokesman demanded, "Is New York a commercial phenomenon or a city?" the answer came swiftly. Speakers for business and financial interests cited the economic and tax gains the city would realize from demolishing the station. A spokesman for the construction industry pointed out that, by a happy coincidence, demolition was planned to begin just as work on the World's Fair concluded, and the politically powerful industry wanted the jobs the project would provide. What was intended to be the clinching statement came from the general manager of the Statler Hilton, across Seventh Avenue from the terminal. The Madison Square Garden project, he enthused, "will show visitors that . . . we are progressing and they should return."

It is late Friday afternoon and very hot and humid. Arriving passengers file through Penn Station's main waiting room, laden with baggage, following signs promising taxis. Steep metal staircases have been erected over the part of the station currently being demolished, and the travelers puff up the steps, flushed and perspiring. They straggle down a maze of temporary partitions. Overhead the sky is visible through gaping holes in the partly dismantled ceiling. Blinking in the sunlight, they spill into a rubble-strewn area on the Thirty-third Street side of the building—or what is left of it. The roofless arches are reminiscent of bombed-out Coventry. Here, there should be cabs, but there are none. The area is called "The Pit," with good reason. The bewildered people mill about like forlorn refugees. A white-haired woman steps into the roadway and peers up the ramp toward Seventh Avenue. A newspaper truck whizzes by, almost hitting her. "Hey," a policeman shouts, "give a man a road! Those trucks 'll kill ya!" She retreats, panic-stricken, and with her husband toils up the ramp, no longer arriving but fleeing. Experienced travelers who can afford it tip redcaps to fetch cabs on the street and ride them back. New York is not kind to the unknowing.

The traveler's predicament is no less brutal on being spilled from the self-opening doors of the city's sleek, modern terminal buildings at Kennedy Airport. On the cab line, it is every man for himself. Well-groomed businessmen, elbowing their way ahead of women and families with children, dogtrot up the ramp to grab the door handles of cabs that are still moving. For their part, some cab drivers, if no patrolman is nearby, will illegally interrogate the would-be passenger as to his destination. If it is not to his liking (i.e., the suburbs rather than Manhattan), he will drive on to pick up a better prospect. This small but ugly breakdown of civilization on the threshold of the city could be prevented by having passengers take numbers and form a line, but New York prefers to introduce the traveler to its ways at the earliest opportunity.

Many of the eighty-four Doric columns that adorned the exterior of Penn Station wound up as landfill in the Secaucus Meadows of New Jersey. But the wreckers were not entirely scornful of the building's defenders. The campaign to preserve

Penn Station brought the offer of a compromise that, in its way, is just as symbolic as the station's destruction. If someone would put up the money, the wreckers proposed to spare some of the columns. These would be moved, quite pointlessly, to a city park.

This scheme has the merit of illustrating the official view of public outdoor space in this cramped city: parks are vacant real estate. It should not be supposed that officials oppose parks; on the contrary, they are vocally for them. It is simply that they do not understand what a real park is. A park is a place that people *use,* not because it is there but because it attracts them. The typical New York park is underused, as the result of what seems a settled official policy: parks should be dull. Because of the official bias in favor of costly building, as opposed to inexpensive maintenance, too many parks that might be used are dirty, vandalized, and unattractive. The ill-planned, antiseptic park and the poorly maintained, un-inviting one are similarly barren of people.

Battery Park, at the tip of Manhattan Island, offers the finest view of the harbor and could be a lively focal point of the city's leisure life. Instead, it is alive only intermittently, as when clerks in the Wall Street area briefly come to sit on the benches and eat their lunches from brown paper bags. In spite of the magnificently dramatic setting, the park, in Jane Jacobs' phrase, resembles "the grounds of an old people's home." A chest-high black iron fence encloses acres of unused grass. The Parks Department long ago laid down the rule that the people must keep off city grass, as though it were an immense private lawn. The fenced-off park is almost inaccessible to pedestrians except at the main entrance near the customs house; once inside, there is little to draw and hold crowds. The excursion boats which encircle Manhattan and take tourists to the Statue of Liberty are offered matter-of-factly, without a trace of flair or showmanship. The Park Department cafeteria is cheerless and institutional. (Imagine what it would be like to eat a fine seafood dinner in a good restaurant that offered the same view.) The city once maintained an aquarium in the park, which drew city families throughout the day. But the aquarium was moved to Coney Island, which, incidentally, has declined sharply in popularity as an amusement center as it has become rough and tawdry. Old and famous Steeplechase Park on the boardwalk has been sold and will be torn down. So disappears another place New Yorkers enjoyed, which our children will never see.

The most successful outdoor public space in the city is Central Park, a miracle of green in the midst of Manhattan's jumbled mass of steel and concrete. The threat here is misuse, and the park is continually under assault by would-be "developers," public and private. Central Park is coveted partly because it's there—vacant real estate—and partly because it has the vitality that comes from public use (although people do not dare use it after dark, except in a few well-lighted places).

If the city will lop off the loveliest corner of the park, opposite the Plaza (and soon within the shadow of the G.M. Building), a place where people naturally stroll, Huntington Hartford stands ready to donate an outdoor restaurant, which, of course, would bear his name. Three blocks away, the neglected southwest corner of the park, adjacent to Columbus Circle, badly needs a pavilion where people might stroll or rest, but a restaurant in that location would not be as successful, nor would it show off the Hartford benefaction to best advantage. (Hartford, as it happens, not long ago built an art museum on Columbus Circle, but it has not notably graced the area.) Another proposal came from a city official who wanted some land for a housing project. Pointing out that his idea would reduce the problem of relocating slum dwellers, he asked that some acreage be chopped off the park's north end, which would be "replaced" by developing parks on city-owned land somewhere else. After all, grass is just grass.

8 To middle-class New York families with children, suburbia continues to appear green with the promise of a better life. Various estimates indicate that between 1950 and 1960 the central core of New York City lost about a million members of the middle-class. In their report on New

York, the architects commented gloomily on the exodus of the city's middle-class population. "The continued mass rejection of this city as a place to live, by a large and significant segment of the population, poses social and economic threats. The new dwelling units and neighborhoods that are being built or planned in the city, with certain notable exceptions, are not the types which will make families move back to town in appreciable numbers. Almost all families who can afford it, except the very rich, reject New York City as a place to bring up children.

"We are forced to recognize," the report continued, "that the public housing program here has seldom produced distinguished or even satisfactory architecture from human and environmental viewpoints. Too many developments are institutional in character, forbiddingly uniform in height and bulk and lacking in the amenities which foster good neighborhoods. What is missing in public housing is generally missing in all our city housing. There is little that gives it life, little to stir our pride."

At election time, New York politicians ritualistically bemoan the shortage of middle-income housing, as though the rate of construction had fallen behind demand and could be satisfied only by building more and bigger projects. In this view, the apartment hunter is merely seeking adequate living space at a price he can afford. But the question of where to live, as everyone knows, is much more complicated than that. New York, surprisingly enough, is beginning to have trouble selling apartments in its publicly aided middle-income housing. Some existing projects have vacancy rates nearing 20 percent in spite of "bargain" rents of about $30 a month a room.

Political and bureaucratic attempts to solve the middle-income housing "shortage" produce results like the Bridge Apartments, which opened in the winter of 1963. These are four thirty-two-story aluminum-clad towers built on air rights over the Manhattan approaches to the George Washington Bridge. The Kratter Corp. acquired the air rights from the city for more than a million dollars. It also received a $17,-700,000 mortgage loan at 4½ percent (covering 90 percent of the project's cost) from the New York State Housing Finance Agency and a 40 percent real-estate tax abatement from the city in order to bring rentals down to an average of $28 a room. Described by the builder's brochure as "a striking new concept in middle-income living," the Bridge Apartments are just another housing project, another vertical filing cabinet for people bearing the tag "middle-income," which is thus defined: the maximum total income allowable for a family of four is seven times the annual rental.

In spite of the agreeably modest rentals, a more artificial environment can scarcely be imagined. The towers overwhelm every building in the vicinity; the project stands separated from the surrounding neighborhood like a forbidding fortress. At eye level along the sidewalks bordering the project are high black walls with tiny wire-mesh windows—the on-site parking garages—which invite the hostility of the area's older residents in the apartment houses across the street. On the roof of each garage, invisible from the street, is a sitting area, described as a "raised loggia," which assures residents of complete isolation. The "loggias" are unshaded and empty. Beneath roars a steady flow of bridge traffic. At rush hours and on summer weekend evenings, traffic stalls and exhaust fumes rise up the sides of the chimney-like towers. "If I lived there," says an expert on air pollution, "I'd order all windows on the highway side of the building to be permanently shut."

In areas of the city where middle-class families might like to live, there is a very real shortage of *decent* housing within their means. Political remedies evade this problem, which is the direct result of political cowardice. Alone among the U.S. metropolitan areas that came under federal rent control during World War II, New York still remains shackled to it, now under city administration. Because of the artificially low rents they pay, tenants whose children have grown and left cling to apartments much larger than they need, thus denying living space to the next generation of young families. Under rent control, the gradual deterioration of buildings (and neighborhoods) is practically guaranteed by the inability of landlords to obtain what they consider an equitable—i.e., competitive—return on their property. The distortions and inequities produced by rent control have long been obvious, but powerful pressure groups hold the club of the "tenants' vote" over City Hall, and the politicians knuckle under. Only a small, timid move in the right direction has been made so far: apartments renting for $250 or more a month have been decontrolled.

Rent control does not apply to new construction; therefore the builders of high-priced "luxury" apartments, as the beneficiaries of artificial scarcity, are strongly in favor of it. Some 70,000 of such dwelling units have been constructed on Manhattan alone in the past five years, and high-rise barracks mushroom throughout the city. Builders have been especially active on the Upper East Side, where a three-room apartment in a new air-conditioned building rents for at least $200 a month. This price buys a relatively convenient location and glossy trimmings, such as uniformed doormen, lavishly decorated lobbies, and music in the elevators, but construction is generally slipshod. The city's building code, now being revised for the first time in nearly thirty years, has not kept up with new materials and labor union "featherbedding" practices. A wall that meets the code's minimum standards for strength and fire resistance may be thin and porous. Through the walls of expensive new apartment buildings can be heard the sounds of neighbors' conversation and flushing toilets. Small rooms and low ceilings are disguised with a sadly transparent gimmick: the terrace or balcony. Row upon row, these small platforms rise up the bleak walls of "luxury" buildings, providing an excellent soot catcher and pigeon roost, but a view of only traffic, rooftops, and other people's terraces. Except that the address is better, the terrace offers at a stiff price little more than the tenement fire escape offered for nothing.

Even after weighing the difficulties of living in the city, many middle-class families might grit their teeth and stay put if it were not for a single, overriding concern: the education of their children. The public school is the secular church of the middle-class—white and Negro alike. The removal of white children from public schools—enrollment in parochial and private schools is 90 percent white—and the flight to the suburbs bear witness to a staggering loss of faith in the city's public school system, which has been all but torn apart over the issue of racial integration. Even without the turmoil this issue has generated, the problems of running a school system embracing 850 schools, almost 47,000 teachers, and more than one million pupils of incredibly heterogeneous backgrounds, under an annual budget of a billion dollars, would strain to the limit the city's genius and resources. With the emotion-charged question of race dominating everything, as it has in recent years, the school system is no longer a "system" at all, but a chaotic battleground, with the children certain to be the ultimate victims. Moreover, the outcome of the integration battle has already been decided. A few statistics reveal that the oft-proclaimed official goal of achieving "racial balance" in the city's elementary and secondary schools is impossible: From 1957 through 1964, Negro enrollment increased 67 per

cent and Puerto Rican 48 percent, while white enrollment dropped 13 percent, to barely more than half of the total—54.5 percent. In 1965, for the first time, there were more Negroes and Puerto Ricans—50.8 percent of the total—enrolled in city elementary schools than whites. By 1975, it has been officially estimated, Negro and Puerto Rican enrollment will exceed 70 percent of the city's total public-school enrollment. In Manhattan, it is already 73 percent.

The plans put forward by the Board of Education offer little hope of disproving the tragic prophecy that the public schools, on which our democratic society is based, will come to serve only part of the public. The only way to achieve a meaningful degree of integration will be to restore the shattered faith of the middle-class in the future of the city's schools; and this will require a period of stability during which priority is given to improving the quality of instruction for all children. This asks patience on the part of frustrated minority groups, and resolution on the part of politically vulnerable educators and public officials. For their part, the frightened middle-class émigrés from the metropolis must face up to the inevitable breakdown of residential segregation as increasing numbers of Negroes and Puerto Ricans claim the chance for what they, too, think is a better life in the suburbs. The movement of middle-class Negro and Puerto Rican families from the city will shift the scene of New York's unavoidable racial confrontation. It seems probable that the most agonizing tests of democratic principle and contrary practice in the next decade will occur, not around the ghettos of the central city, but in the far-flung suburbs.

9 The borough of Queens, just across the East River from Manhattan and the fastest growing of New York's five boroughs, receives much of the city's fleeing middle-class population. Here families find apartments at prices they can manage, at the sacrifice of amenities. The scene along the main east-west axis, Queens Boulevard, is one of unrelieved dullness as apartment houses march in close order into the horizon. Easily the most awesome middle-income project, built without any sort of government assistance, is Lefrak City. Ultimately this huge complex will consist of twenty-four eighteen-story brick towers housing 25,000 persons. In advertising the opening of its latest building ("The Wellington"), Lefrak City promises "a totally new approach to total living" that makes the project a self-contained community. An air-conditioned, two-bedroom apartment, containing 1,080 square feet of space, rents for $220 a month, but price and swimming pools are not the main attractions of Lefrak City. Its greatest promise is release from the ordeal of long-distance commuting. Just south of the project lies the

Long Island Expressway (aptly dubbed the world's longest parking lot), and Nassau- and Suffolk-bound drivers, as they sit stalled in the nightly bumper-to-bumper jams, face signs like this: "If we lived here, Daddy, you'd be home now."

Many weary breadwinners have sold their split-levels and moved their families to Lefrak City, which is within walking distance of the Independent Subway. This is the lesson of Lefrak City and smaller projects throughout Queens: New Yorkers will gladly accept ugliness—indeed, they become blind to it—for the sake of relative convenience. Lefrak City, in spite of its advertised "galaxy of Happy Life innovations," is as ugly as mass-production building can make it; from soot-darkened windows one can see only streets and the expressway, an overcrowded (triple-session) public school, parking lots, and other apartment buildings. There is, however, a super-market at the door—not, as in suburbia, ten minutes away by car; and a housewife need walk only two blocks to rummage through the heaped counters at Alexander's department store. Most important of all, Manhattan lies only a half hour away by subway; this virtue alone redeems every flaw of the environment.

But, alas, the lure of living close to the subway proves false. For thousands upon thousands of other people also want to live close to the subway, and when they come together at the rush hours, the crowding is inhuman.

It is half-past seven in the morning. The first wave of Man-

hattan office workers is leaving Lefrak City and the surrounding projects. They walk the long blocks past the chain-wire fences of the municipal parking lots to the subway station at Woodhaven Boulevard. Many of them are not due at their desks until nine o'clock, but they travel early to avoid the crush that will build steadily in the next hour. Now it is possible to board the local easily and even get a seat for the ride to the express stop at Roosevelt Avenue in Jackson Heights.

By a few minutes past eight the parking lots around the Woodhaven Boulevard station are filling up rapidly as cars stream from the expressway. Buses filled to capacity pull up and disgorge their passengers. Now the subway platform is packed six deep with people waiting impassively. As the local arrives, they surge forward, merging, pushing, straining. Some clutch newspapers, but they cannot move, much less read. At Roosevelt Avenue, the express trains arriving from Jamaica, Kew Gardens, and Forest Hills are jammed to the doors, but somehow more bodies squeeze inside. By eight-thirty the crowd at Woodhaven Boulevard backs up the stairs. Those in the rear files must wait for one and perhaps two locals before they can wedge themselves aboard. At the stations all along Queens Boulevard, these scenes are repeated morning and evening. Each rider drops only a fifteen-cent token in the turnstile, but that is the smallest part of what this degrading experience costs him.

Because the city has failed in its responsibility, no demand the office worker faces during an ordinary day approaches the physical and emotional strain of getting to and from work.* There are too many riders on the Jamaica line of the IND subway and the Flushing line of the IRT subway—at least 22,000 too many, by the Planning Commission's count—and this overloading will worsen. Only now, fully ten years too late, is the city undertaking new subway construction. Conditions are equally bad on Manhattan's Lexington Avenue line, the only subway serving the booming east-midtown area, which also handles much of the traffic to the financial district. The gross inadequacy of present rapid transit facilities is merely part of the penalty for the city's uncoordinated growth. Looming ahead is the Planning Commission's estimate that, within the next two decades, some 45,000 additional peak-hour commuters will be fighting their way to Manhattan from Queens, Nassau, and Suffolk.

In spite of his daily ordeal, the subway rider is at least assured that the subway will continue to operate. Railroad commuters in the metropolitan area, who suffer ordeals of their own, have no such assurance. The bankrupt New Haven Railroad, which hauls 26,000 commuters daily, has threatened

---

* Anyone who doubts that city life inspires masochism should ponder this observation by the Planning Commission: "Experience on the Queens Boulevard locals and other subway lines shows conclusively that New Yorkers will not voluntarily get off a crowded express to ride a less crowded local that is almost as fast; they will ride the local only when there is no more standing room on the express." Perhaps wary New Yorkers dare not risk dashing across the platform only to have the doors shut in their faces.

to discontinue its passenger service. The commuter railroads of New Jersey are in dismal condition. The bankrupt Long Island Rail Road, the world's busiest commuter line, has repeatedly raised fares and cut service in spite of various forms of government aid. In order to keep it running, New York State recently purchased the Long Island for $65 million, which is not a "solution" to its woes but only the beginning of one. Transportation in the metropolitan area can be rationally planned and efficiently operated only on a regional basis, as the states of New York, New Jersey, and Connecticut recognized by forming the Tri-State Transportation Committee. Lacking funds and real power, the committee is little more than a good intention. On its own, New York State has created the Metropolitan Commuter Transportation Authority, an enormously powerful and almost completely independent agency to deal with commuter services into New York City by train, bus, ferry, and plane. The authority may become the nucleus of a coordinated network of commuter transportation throughout the metropolitan region.

However, this offers no immediate hope to the suffering riders on the subway, which has not been integrated into the new authority. At the cost of modest amounts of imagination and money, something could be done fairly quickly. The Long Island's tracks and tunnels within the city are not used to capacity during rush hours; therefore the Planning Commission proposes that subway trains be operated at reduced fares on its lines, which would ease the crowding on the subway. It is a sound idea, an obvious one, yet several years after it was first proposed, nothing has come of it.

10 Those residents of Queens who endure much to live close to the subway have had the misfortune of coming a generation too late. When the subway first pushed into the undeveloped borough, city dwellers who moved there could enjoy what seems to them in retrospect "a golden era." The new rapid transportation opened up living space faster than people could use it. It did not seem to matter then that the land was poorly used: Manhattan's gridiron street patterns were imposed on rolling hills and the small houses in the new "developments" were squeezed together unimaginatively. There was so much land that a property owner possessing only a 60-by-100 lot did not feel in the least cramped. And between the subdivisions lay farms and fields of wild flowers and woods in which boys could build huts.

Immediately before and after World War II the steady expansion of Long Island's highway system kept open the opportunity for people to leapfrog the developed areas and enjoy open country that still lay within reasonable commuting distance of Manhattan. Year by year, new home seekers have pressed eastward through Nassau and into Suffolk County, where commuting to Manhattan takes as much as four hours a day. The office worker who must make the 60-mile trek from Port Jefferson each day realizes acutely how tarnished is the lure of open land. Slumped behind his newspaper on the Long Island Rail Road, stalled in his car on the expressway, he is no longer the beneficiary of transportation, but the victim of its depleted promise. Before Queens, other parts of the city —Brooklyn, the Bronx—enjoyed similar "golden eras" between the introduction of improved transportation and the intensive development of land. But now the land has almost been used up.

The last breathing space left within the city is Staten Island —officially known as the borough of Richmond—which is separated from Manhattan by a five-mile stretch of Upper New York Bay. So long as the island was linked to New York only by ferry, land and homes were inexpensive, and the island kept its predominantly rural character. But in November, 1964, the Verrazano Bridge across the Narrows connected Staten Island with Brooklyn, a physical link that has important psychological implications. At the ground breaking five years earlier, Robert Moses had called the island "this one remaining unspoiled borough." The despoliation is now well advanced.

Anticipating a surge of population across the bridge, small speculative builders have thrown up cheaply constructed,

overpriced frame houses on every available tract in the built-up northern half of the island. As Jerome Zukosky, real-estate writer on the *Herald Tribune* has observed, it is as though "nothing learned in a century of surburban land planning could be applied in New York City in 1964." Row upon row, huddled together on forty-foot lots, the identical wooden boxes line the long gridiron streets. Every amenity (and many a necessity) has been grudged by the rapacious land exploiters. On many houses, there is scarcely a trace of such durable building materials as brick and concrete; the crude wooden steps and landings recall the barracks of World War II. The structures seem to sag with age even before they are occupied. The plots are bare and treeless, there are no play spaces, often no driveways and garages. These builders and their financial and political allies are producing, not suburban housing, but only ugly "slurbs," thus robbing a rising generation of young families of their chance for a "golden era" of decent living conditions close to the heart of the city.

This chance still exists on part of Staten Island, thanks to citizens who fought to preserve it. Much of the land in the undeveloped southern half of the island is owned by the city and provides an unusual opportunity for planning true communities from the ground up. The key to this opportunity is the Annadale-Huguenot tract, embracing 1,080 acres on the south shore, which has been a battleground since 1961. The story illustrates the extreme vulnerability of the public interest in New York when it collides with vested political and commercial interests.

Speculators invaded the Annadale-Huguenot area during the land boom of the 1920's dividing it into long, rectangular blocks and small building lots. The city drew up street maps based on the familiar gridiron. But the collapse of the boom and the onset of the depression wiped out speculators and lot buyers alike, with the result that taxes went unpaid and the city took over most of the land. For a generation, it lay vacant and wooded, the only streets dirt tracks, the few houses mostly summer bungalows. But the pattern of lot lines, streets, and utility easements had never been "finally mapped." In 1961, these original maps were submitted to the City Planning Commission, which seized upon the opportunity to replan the Annadale-Huguenot area as a model suburb within the city, substituting for the monotonous gridiron a pattern of loop streets and cul-de-sacs following the natural contours of the land. Drawing on the design of the pioneering planned community of Radburn, New Jersey, the commission envisioned clusters of houses built around a chain of small parks leading to the bay front, schools and stores. The city's urban-renewal power would be used to acquire the 154 privately-owned acres within the tract, most of which were undeveloped. After replanning, which would set aside space for schools, libraries, and other public uses, the city would sell the remaining land to private developers for construction of houses of good quality in a variety of sizes and prices. The economics of the plan were attractive: the commission estimated that the city would easily recover what it spent to acquire the privately owned land. The commission unveiled the Annadale-Huguenot plan in the fall of 1962, expecting its obvious merits to produce swift and enthusiastic public support.

Instead the plan aroused loud opposition, which grew violent when, in April, 1963, the commission designated the area as an open-lands project under the Urban Renewal Act. The opposition came from an unlikely but effective dual alliance: some residents of the area, who wanted nothing to change in their rural preserve (the words "urban renewal" evoked menacing images of apartment buildings, public housing, Negroes and other outsiders); and real-estate men and speculative builders, who wanted to build as many houses as possible, as quickly as possible, on the basis of the pre-depression maps. Nor was there anything approaching unity of purpose within the city government itself. Regardless of the Planning Commission's plans, the Real Estate Department, eager to turn city-owned land into badly needed cash, viewed the Annadale-Huguenot tract as nothing more than a scarce commodity that might bring, in piecemeal auction sales to speculators, at least $10 million. Richmond's Borough President Albert V. Maniscalco, who at first had assured the commission of his support for the project, tested the political breeze and quickly reversed himself. He asked the commission to abandon its plans, but

93

was refused. "Failure to take advantage of this great opportunity," wrote the acting chairman of the commission, "will prove a mistake that will haunt not only Annadale but the entire borough for generations to come." Unmoved, Maniscalco, using pleas that are too easily imagined, finally persuaded Mayor Wagner to back up his request. The Mayor directed the commission to rescind the Annadale-Huguenot project and prepare final city maps of the area, opening the way for sale of the land. The announcement from City Hall was released on a Friday afternoon, so it would be buried in the lightly read Saturday papers.

Typically, Mayor Wagner did not put the plan to death openly, but instead favored slow death by frustration, which would conceal the hand of the executioner. He directed the commission to try to replan the area without using urban renewal, a plainly impossible task. But the commission took up the assignment and spent the next eight months trying to carry it out. As pressures built up to release the land for sale, the maddeningly deliberate pace of bureaucracy, which so often contributes to the city's ills, now worked to its advantage. For a group of citizens used these months of official inaction to organize the "Ad Hoc Committee on Open Lands on Staten Island," which for the first time mobilized public support for the Annadale-Huguenot project. The prime movers—a thirty-six-year-old lawyer for Union Carbide Corp., a newspaperman, a graphic arts designer, and a Wall Street corporation lawyer—also blocked sale of the city-owned land through a suit filed in the Supreme Court in Manhattan. At a public hearing last March, the Planning Commission was expected to kill its project and release the land for sale. But the Ad Hoc Committee staged an impressive protest, which the planners were privately pleased to heed. People living within the Annadale-Huguenot area at last wanted the project badly enough to fight for it.

Now the politicians did an about-face. Late in April, Mayor Wagner announced that, on the basis of consultations with various city officials, he believed the city should "move as expeditiously as possible to apply for funds to plan this area as a model community." The project still has to clear several obstacles, including approval by the Board of Estimate, but at least hope of eventual success has been restored. The Mayor's self-reversal was hardly "leadership" and the last-minute defeat of a manifestly bad land-use policy was hardly "progress," leaving the city right where it had been two years earlier. But in New York, alas, "progress" is often measured, not by what is accomplished to advance the city's well-being, but rather by what has been prevented that would have hastened the city's decline.

11 Who runs New York? The temptation is strong to reply: nobody. Many serious-minded voters, who have all but given up hope of having responsive, efficient city government, believe they live within an unfathomably complex system, which mysteriously runs on momentum and periodically collapses into anarchy. Most New Yorkers probably would reply that the Mayor runs New York, at least in theory. A few years ago the City Charter was revised, the first such overhaul in a quarter-century, and the power of the Mayor's office was greatly enhanced. Acting City Administrator Maxwell Lehman, in an article on the city's power structure in a scholarly journal, has written with the authority of intimate knowledge that "the powers of New York City's Mayor are immense—probably greater than those of any other local official in the world."

Lehman defines power as "the ability to get things accomplished," and this the Mayor must have, but there is no correlation between the extent of his power and the quality of municipal government. What counts for much more than power is the will to use it. A weak, indecisive man, no matter how powerful on paper, will be a weak Mayor; while a strong energetic individual, improvising with the power he has, may govern effectively. If the Mayor will not act, the concentration of power in his hands, accomplished through charter revision with the aim of streamlining city government, becomes a formidable deterrent to action at any level of government.

Wet paint!
J.J. MASSOLINI
NEW YORK N Y

New Yorkers are not fearful of seeing enormous power pass into the hands of the rare official who regularly fulfills his promises of action. As the spectacular career of Robert Moses shows, they will allow an able, strong-willed man to gain such inordinate power that he rules as an absolute despot, beyond the reach of the ballot or even public opinion. Until a few years ago, Moses was simultaneously head of the city parks, the Triborough Bridge and Tunnel Authortiy, the New York State Power Authority, the State Council of Parks, the Mayor's Committee on Slum Clearance, and Coordinator of City Construction—which is too much authority for any one man. For the past two years he has concentrated his energies on the World's Fair, stubbornly keeping admission prices high in the face of dismal attendance and blistering anyone who questions his infallibility. A tyrant is no less a tyrant for being public-spirited (by his lights); and his successes cannot conceal the failure of popular self-government that produced him.

The last Mayor of New York to give the impression that he was on top of the job was, of course, the almost legendary Fiorello H. La Guardia. The vacuum at City Hall dates from the departure of the "Little Flower" in 1945. Since then, New York has suffered through a succession of incompetents and self-servers who have rattled around in the enormous job of running the world's greatest city—with the exception of the incumbent. Mayor Robert F. Wagner, who will retire next year after serving three four-year terms, might have proven big enough for the job, but he never dared measure himself against its challenges.

Wagner is decent, well-intentioned, and quite popular—so popular, in spite of the city's decline, that there is little doubt he could have been re-elected to an unprecedented fourth term if he had chosen to run. But this popularity, securely based on the city's monolithic Democratic majority, is evidence of the Mayor's sad failure to run the risks of leading. As his long tenure draws to a close, Wagner stands to be forgotten by the public but remembered by other politicians as the man who raised their professional habit of avoiding responsibility to the level of artistry. Almost invariably, his response to crisis has been to temporize by hoarding his power and appointing a powerless committee whose report will not be acted upon. In no other city have so many urgent problems been studied so exhaustively with so little visible effect.

Yet at least one of the Mayor's abilities has been demonstrated again and again. It is the ability to maintain, with engaging sincerity, that he is firmly in charge when things have clearly gotten out of control. For example, in offering his executive budget for the fiscal year 1965-66, Wagner sternly declared: "I am determined that economy shall be the watchword of this administration." He then proceeded to outline economy measures, such as denying high officials their chauffeur-driven limousines and cutting back staff and budget in certain facilities, such as the Betts Avenue waste heat plant.

The City Planning Commission, which ought to be among the most influential agencies, felt Wagner's economizing axe, being cut back by $114,000 to a budget of less than a million dollars. It was a virtuoso performance on Wagner's part, not so much in the details of his economy drive as in his grand assertion that a spirit of rigorous thrift animated the budget he presented. For it was a staggeringly irresponsible budget, the largest in the city's history, calling for expenditures of $3.9 billion, and it marked the largest annual increase in spending, $493 million more than was spent in 1964-65.

The plain fact is that municipal spending is out of control and the world's richest city lives in a state of chronic bankruptcy. Under Wagner, the city budget has more than doubled, until only the federal government's is larger, but New York cannot finance its deficits as painlessly as Washington. It must borrow and repay. As this is written, the city spends $1,500,000 daily to carry its debt—or more than it spends each day for fire, police, and sanitation services combined. Yet there is to be additional debt incurred to close the huge gap between anticipated city spending and revenues. Under a "borrow-now, repay-later" scheme, which has been branded fiscally irresponsible by his own Controller, Wagner will have the city issue $256 million in bonds to pay current expenses while waiting for the state legislature and the voters in a statewide referendum to give the city the authority to raise real-estate taxes at least 20 percent. The referendum cannot be held until the fall of 1966, at the earliest, and the voters may say no. Even before then, an anticipated $350-million revenue gap in 1966 will make new taxes necessary—if new ones can be devised (and tolerated) in this tax-ridden city. In 1963-64, New York boosted its sales tax to 4 percent, which drove business away from the city while failing to produce expected revenues. (The tax is now 5 percent, shared 60-40 by the city and state.) Clearly visible on the horizon are a city payroll tax or a surcharge on the city resident's state income tax; the latter might have been imposed this year were it not for the mayoralty election. Confirmation of New York's worsening financial plight came this summer when two leading agencies, Dun & Bradstreet and Moody's, downgraded the city's credit rating, which will make borrowing more costly. Moody's noted "increasing evidence" that the city has succumbed to "the pressures of special interests and minority groups, thus permitting spending to get out of hand."

New York illustrates in countless ways how the power to tax, when abused, turns self-destructive. Obviously, oppressive taxation discourages expansion of small businesses and therefore causes shrinkage of the labor market among unskilled and semiskilled workers, who make up the majority of the city's more than 200,000 unemployed. It is far more costly to maintain the jobless and "make" work for them than it would be to reduce spending and refrain from job-destroying taxation. But it is asking too much disinterested logic of Democratic politicians to suggest that they create jobs by cutting the swollen city payroll.

In spite of its opaque language, the Mayor's budget message expresses a tragedy as poignant as any dramatist might contrive. We are told, in effect, that certain fantastic expenditures will grow more fantastic; that they simply cannot be controlled nor can alternatives be devised. For example, welfare spending will increase $75 million this fiscal year, to a total of just under a half *billion* dollars, and here is the Mayor's explanation: "The strongest force in the upward surge of our expenditure requirements is the plight of that major sector of our population which, until now, has lacked equal access to, and opportunity for, significant participation in the benefits of urban life and living. Many of these New Yorkers have long been denied both equal treatment and equal opportunity. Lacking education and skills, they have found no functional place in our economy. Instead, many of them have been a charge against it. The cost of their maintenance (especially that of the children and the aged) is a factor which defies limitation or control. Under the law, we have no alternative but to maintain the needy."

The note of optimism ("until now") is unsupported and unconvincing. Few of the half million persons receiving welfare payments can look forward to finding a "functional place" in the city's economy in the near future. The poor and the taxpayers alike are walking a cruel, hopeless treadmill, which annually becomes more crowded and costly to keep running. For each case the Welfare Department closes, it has been reported, three or four new ones are opened. The department pays its overworked investigators, who must be college graduates, only $5,750 a year to start—less than the city pays laborers. They are condemned to toil within a mechanical, bureaucratic system that demands evidence in quadruplicate of its futility. It is shocking, but not really surprising, that four out of ten of the new investigators quit within the first year. Last spring, seven thousand welfare investigators, defying a state law forbidding strikes by public employees, staged a month-long walkout to protest their low pay, poor morale, and impossible working conditions. Their grievances were just, yet in their frustration the strikers saw no alternative but to press their demands at the expense of the needy, thus exposing the sham of a system that assures no one's "welfare."

The city's new "Attack on Poverty" program calls for spending $72 million ($27 million from the federal government) and is intended, in the Mayor's words, "to enable the poor to help themselves." Before that can happen, however, the poor will have to wait indefinitely while the politicians help *themselves,* turning the "Attack on Poverty" into a defense of their power. No matter how catchy the name chosen or extravagant the promises, every program that attempts to reduce poverty within the cynical, corrupt framework of municipal politics is merely a variation on the custodial handout and foredoomed to failure. This summer, the city and federal governments are spending millions of dollars in "crash" programs aimed at creating 20,000 jobs for unemployed youths—when there are an estimated 70,000 jobless young people. Only within a dynamically expanding metropolitan economy can significant numbers of the unemployed (and *under*employed) get off the treadmill of the dole and gain a chance of becoming self-sufficient. But the economy of New York offers opportunity only to the relatively well off: a skilled office worker can find a better job; the unskilled or semiskilled worker can't find any job at all. By 1970, it has been estimated, almost two-thirds of the city's youths between fifteen and twenty-four years of age will be Negroes and Puerto Ricans, most of them with meager skills.

It was not until 1962 that the city got around to creating a Department of Commerce and Industrial Development, thanks mainly to an extremely public-spirited New Yorker, Louis B. Broido, the department's commissioner. Broido, formerly executive vice president of Gimbels, serves at a salary of a dollar a year, which the city, typically, neglects to pay him. His department is expected to help find jobs for New York's unemployed, to stem the flight of small businesses (and the shrinkage of the labor market), and to attract new businesses to the city. To accomplish all this, the department's budget for the current fiscal year is a pitiful $768,000, of which almost half is earmarked for a bureau that drums up conventions and encourages tourism. The department has a staff of only forty-two, including just one economist. Its entire

109

budget represents less than *one-tenth of one percent* of the municipal budget.

New York is atrociously governed in large measure because the Democratic party has long enjoyed a secure monopoly of political power. With only a couple of interruptions, it has held City Hall since the present five-borough form of municipal organization was introduced more than sixty years ago. Of course, New York would be no better governed if Republicans had enjoyed a similar extended sway. Not the party, but the nature of the human political animal guarantees that one-party rule will be misrule. One-party rule ensures the rise of men who are preoccupied with getting power for no better reason than to deny it to their rivals, and who need not do anything except defend it. No necessity exists for the politician to use power intelligently in the public interest, while every instinct tells him this is foolish and risky.

The slavish loyalty of the city's voters to the Democratic party, reflected in a 3-to-1 preference in registration, ensures that municipal government will be remote from the people and unresponsive to their needs. As far as the politicians are concerned, the number of people who count is very small. For example, the Mayor, while ignoring the needs of hundreds of thousands of wage earners who automatically vote Democratic, must be unfailingly attentive to the wishes of the man who wields the "labor vote," Harry Van Arsdale, president of the city's AFL-CIO Central Labor Council. New York suffers union bosses who make Jimmy Hoffa seem the soul of sweet reasonableness. By threatening to immobilize New Yorkers on New Year's Eve, when his union's contracts expire, blustering Mike Quill, of the Transport Workers, has run the city's transit operating deficit up to $33 million this year. Coldly egotistical Bert Powers, of the Printers, who led the disastrous 114-day strike in 1962-63, seems indifferent to the likelihood that newspapers will die because he will not allow them to break with antiquated production methods. The list could be extended indefinitely. Yet, curiously enough, while New York wears the union label, the workers who need unions most, unskilled Negroes and Puerto Ricans, are largely neglected by organizers; and when minority groups press for admission to skilled craft unions, they are rebuffed.

Mayor Wagner sometimes has had to make abject public obeisance, practically turning the city over to the bosses, as when Van Arsdale spearheaded a strong-arm campaign to organize the city's cab drivers. While goon squads smashed windshields, slashed tires, and threatened drivers and passengers, cabs disappeared from the streets and thousands were inconvenienced. The attitude of union leaders resembles the public-be-damned outlook of the 19th Century robber barons. During a violent one-day strike last spring, a radio reporter asked Van Arsdale how it happened that a dozen members of his electrical worker's union had been arrested during a *taxi* strike. Van Arsdale shoved the microphone away and snarled:

"Get out of here!" Then he entered Madison Square Garden to appear at a strike rally side by side with the smiling Mayor.

12 With Mayor Wagner's announcement of his retirement, the prospects of electing a "reform" Mayor this fall are brighter than at any time in the past generation. And in Congressman John V. Lindsay, the earnest and ambitious Republican representative of Manhattan's "silk stocking" district, who has abandoned the inept clubhouse politicians of his party to campaign as an independent, New York has a potentially effective Mayor. However, a Lindsay victory would not, at a stroke, realize any of the hopes contained in the word "reform." It is a rather old-fashioned word, carried over from a simpler day when the problems of the city could be reduced to the fact that crooked politicians were brazenly stealing City Hall brick by brick; and the obvious solution, as outraged leading citizens saw it, was to throw the rascals out. Nowadays, outrage has become unfashionable, and only the grossest scandal arouses a twitch of public indignation.

The true scandal of New York is that the city has been getting the kind of government it deserves. With some honorable exceptions, those who should be the leading citizens have turned their backs on the city—an example followed

112

literally and massively by the middle ranks of the population in their evacuation to the suburbs. It can be argued that rejection produced rejection; that the failure of leadership deadens public morale and spreads despair. The fact remains that the corruption destroying New York is the dry rot of civic indifference, which is beyond the reach of political "reform."

Politicians, however horrendously they perform, are limited in the damage they can do by the extent of their power. The decisive power in New York is not political, but economic, and its limits cannot be discerned. Whole sections of the city are tacitly understood to fall within the sphere of influence of men wielding such power. Leaders in business, labor, and other fields, for example, are attempting to impose a new order on the area below Canal Street. Key elements in their grand design are the Lower Manhattan Expressway and the World Trade Center, projects that are directly beneficial to their interests. Self-interest lies behind almost every municipal enterprise in which businessmen *actively* involve themselves. Of inactive participants, there is no shortage. Just as corporations give generously but impersonally to charity, so prominent men lend their names to civic organizations, committees, and commissions, often at the request of the Mayor, but do not deeply involve themselves. They are not really expected to. It is sufficient proof of civic responsibility to appear on the letterhead, pay dues, and sign the report written by the executive secretary.

Membership in civic organizations in New York runs heavily to business and professional men—lawyers, bankers, insurance executives, retailers, real-estate operators—whose financial interests are directly related to the city. Such a parochial base of leadership may be sufficient in a Pittsburgh, a Dallas, or even a Chicago, but it is too narrow for a metropolis performing the unique function of New York. New York is only incidentally a regional center of America; its chief role is to serve as the marketplace of the nation and the world. It is everyone's city and therefore no one's special responsibility. The hundreds of corporations with headquarters here ignore New York while lavishing attention on smaller U.S. communities where only a handful of corporations may be represented. It might almost be laid down as a rule that the civic spirit of the average U.S. corporation is proportional to its visibility in a given community. Vast and diverse New York offers the opportunity to hide, and corporations generally, to their discredit and New York's disadvantage, have taken it.

While relatively few New York businessmen wield far-reaching public power, on the order of, say, David Rockefeller of the Chase Manhattan Bank, most possess it in some degree, usually without realizing it. Affluence and position protect them against the effects of their lack of civic interest—and even against an awareness of the ramifications of their attitudes and decisions. The ordinary New York office worker, convinced of the futility of individual protest against his environment, lacking access to the institutional economic power that could bring improvement, is alienated from the city by force of circumstance. New York is where he works; he lives elsewhere, and there he expends his civic energies. The man far above him on the corporate ladder, who perhaps lives in an expensive East Side Manhattan cooperative, walks to work, and enjoys the amenities available to the wealthy, stands aloof from the actual life of the city by choice. Preoccupied with business and accustomed to applying only commercial values in his decision making, he unconsciously accepts the concept of the city as a work environment only. At the same time he wonders, without a sense of self-contradiction, why New York is such a mess.

"This is a violent, noisy, dirty city. The dirtiest I've ever seen," complained a New York executive, one of several whom *Fortune* interviewed not long ago. "If you want to live comfortably here, you've got to insulate yourself as much as possible."

Again and again, in conversations with more than a score of executives (and many of their wives), this refrain was heard: "If we didn't have enough money to insulate ourselves, New York would be unbearable." How much is "enough"? What with high rents or maintenance charges on cooperatives, servants' salaries, vacations and entertaining, these upper-class New Yorkers decided that a couple needed about $3,000 a month *after taxes* to live comfortably in Manhattan. It was estimated that it costs at least $3,000 a year to maintain a child in the city, with the largest single expense being tuition in a private school. (The public schools are regarded as "impossible.") Many of these executives had once lived in suburbia, and were glad to be free of the daily grind of commuting and the hectic social life on weekends. They found Manhattan "restful" by comparison and relished the opportunities it offered for spontaneous relaxation. ("We can go to the theatre without making a deal out of it, and I don't feel like hell the next day.") Most of all, these men cherished the privacy of the city. After working long hours (at least fifty a week), they were reasonably sure of being left alone. To avoid occasions of obligation, most admitted they did not attend church regularly. "My life is so filled with meetings and duties during the week," explained one, "that, come Sunday, I'm through." The choice of Manhattan as a place to live was based wholly on personal taste and convenience, and implied no commitment to the city. On the contrary, the refusal to commit oneself was conscious and unyielding. Except for charitable organizations and institutions, in which several of their wives were active (sometimes with an eye to social prestige), these men shunned involvement in civic affairs. Some actively discouraged it among their subordinates. ("There's no reason for them to give time to extraneous things. We want their time.") In most cases, their friends were drawn from business, usually from within their own specialized worlds, and many lived nearby in the wealthy enclave of Manhattan's Upper East Side.

The way of life revealed in these interviews, while comfortable, is totally insular. Most of these executives worked in other cities on their way to the corner office in the New York head-quarters. As rising young men, they did not—*could not*—in-sulate themselves from the smaller communities. "In Cincin-nati, I felt some peripheral responsibility as a businessman to get involved in civic affairs," recalled one executive. "In the company here in New York nobody has the slightest interest in my personal life. In the smaller city one's personal and business lives get all mixed up. Here my wife and I are freer."

This man and others like him believe they have earned their freedom—and who would deny them the rewards of their hard work? They, and the corporations they lead, are free to believe that they can exist apart from the unpleasantness and ugliness of the city, exploiting it yet securely withdrawn from it. But the "insulation" around these illusions is wearing perilously thin. Some businessmen realize this, and are making a fresh commitment to New York. The Committee of Fourteen, com-posed of top executives, has been organized to stimulate New York's economy and expand job opportunities for unskilled and semiskilled workers. The new Committee for Action on the Commuter Railroad Problem is seeking a "permanent so-lution," based on area-wide planning and government action. Through such groups new lines of personal, informal contact may be established between business and government.

But these hopeful signs and good intentions are few and feeble in the face of the city's mounting crisis. More and more,

New York has the look of a place that has been abandoned, physically and psychologically, by those citizens who might somehow bring about its rescue. No program of reform contains the smallest hope of success unless these citizens experience a change of heart—it is as simple and as bleak as that. Of what must this indispensable changed attitude consist? Nothing more or less than the conviction, born of whatever individual motive, that the place is worth the bother after all.

Index

Index

RICHARD J. WHALEN was born in 1935 in New York City and was graduated with honors from Queens College in 1957. He began his career as a reporter for the *Richmond* (Va.) *News Leader,* and within two years was named associate editor of the newspaper. Returning to New York, Mr. Whalen joined *Time* magazine as a contributing editor, writing on national affairs, and was later an editorial writer for *The Wall Street Journal.* In 1962, he became an associate editor of *Fortune* magazine. He is the author of *The Founding Father: The Story of Joseph P. Kennedy,* which was a national bestseller for more than six months and has recently won extraordinary acclaim in England ("one of the great modern biographies," commented the *Spectator).* Mr. Whalen and his wife and two children live on Long Island.